II
Passion:
The Gemini Project

PassionPoet
Robert R. Gibson

Copyright © 2024 Robert R. Gibson

First published 2019

All rights reserved.

ISBN: 978-976-96544-6-4

No part of this publication is to be copied, transmitted, or recorded in any form, except for small snippets for the purpose of review, without the prior, express, written permission of the author.

Editing / Book Layout by
Passionate Words Editing Services

(IG @passionate.words.editing246)

Dedication

This book is dedicated to those lovers of poetry and wordplay that have supported me faithfully through the years. This book is dedicated to those who have wondered who am I outside of the sex – as I always say in my signature piece "Passion is more than sex…" and this anthology will prove that. Yes I intend to bring the sexy, but there will also be other sides to me that I hope you enjoy. This book – is dedicated to YOU!

Acknowledgements

First and foremost I want to thank the Almighty Divine, giver of creativity and sensuality. In truth, spirituality and sexuality are linked … I prove it over and over in my writing!

I want to acknowledge my **EroticEmpire** group, who have been instrumental in getting me my platform to behave 'inappropriately' for so many years!

I want to acknowledge Sandra 'Seawoman' Sealy for her unending support for me as a writer, who saw my potential from the days of VOICES Writer's Collective and who gave me my first feature ever as 'The Looooooove Man' before I became PassionPoet. She also put me on to my amazing Nigerian graphic artist Emily, who assisted me with my cover!

I also want to acknowledge my former protégé Mariposa, who is doing amazing work on her own along with being a major supporter of my work.

I want to acknowledge those who have ever heard or read any of my spoken word pieces, either live or recorded, and anyone who has ever bought any one of my books! Thank you immensely!

Table of Contents

Part 1: PLEASURE — 11

Pleasure	12
Nymph	14
Foreplay (1)	15
Work of Art (2)	17
Mutuality	19
Foreplay (2)	21
Tasting The Glory	23
Instantly Wet	25
Open Up	26
Muse	28
Warmth	30
Delicious	32
Inspired	34
Magic	36
Sensual Lullaby	38
Emotional Voyeurism	40
Receptivity	42
Telepathy	44
Temptation	46

Morning Fragrance	48
Dark Sugar	49
Pink Poetry	51
Playtime	53
Morning Conversation	55
Touched	57
Alchemy	59
Intentions	60
Erotic Poetry	62
Waiting	64
Thirst	66
Filthy	68
I Want a Hug	70
Breakfast in Bed	71
Pied Piper	73
Surprise	75
Waiting	77

Part 2: PAIN — 79

Call Me for Prayer	80
Gambler	83
Homicide	84
Battle-Weary	86

Mirage	88
Momentary Clarity	90
Moving On	92
Ooooops!	94
Package	96
Reality or Fallacy?	99
Tactile	101
Tears	103
Tempered Glass	105
The Fight	107
The Wind of a Thousand Whispers	109
Vigil (1)	111
Vigil (2)	113
Kryptonite	114
Morning Thoughts	115
Persona Non Grata	116
About the Author	119

Part 1:
PLEASURE

Pleasure

I'm here
Solely
For your
Pleasure

Not thinking
Selfishly
At all

My goal isn't
My own
Nut

But

My desire
Is to light
The fire

Under your
Panties

Until the
Scalding
Heat

Makes you
Strip

And spread
Your thighs

Wide

Summoning
Any gust
Of cooling breeze

To

Caress your clit

Just call
My tongue
A zephyr...

Nymph

Goddess curves sinful in sensuality,
Brown skin simmering chocolate in winking sunlight,
I am struck dumb by your beauty;
As I feel like I impose with my presence -
Happening upon you suddenly
Shrouded in sea of blue.
Naked body curled into a sensual ball
Of self-pleasure.
I am drawn to the sinuous curve of your spine
Your hips and ass draw my stare
As the dark flow of your locs hides visage from view
Moans of pleasure merge:
Your voice and my thoughts.

Foreplay (1)

Wordplay
my foreplay

whispering words
softly

Making intellect
stand
Erect

Ready to
penetrate
your moistness

With phrases
as
Synapses fire

Exploding fireworks

Hair follicles
Stand
On end

And as I slip

slowly inside
your
Moistened lips

My heated words
Make you
Convulse.

Work of Art (2)

Just look at you standing there: posing.
Smiling from ear to ear as your arms are outstretched, just so, in perpetual welcome.
Statuesque neck craned in invite, shoulders flexed and breasts perfectly formed.
Your nipples invite me – beg me – to touch them. To feel them pebble under my probing
Skin smooth, marble glistening in the light of my investigation.
And I continue my examination:
Down smooth stomach chiseled with the precision of the artisan;
Legs muscled and toned, slightly parted, as you present your joy;
And I want to run into your arms and hold you, get lost in your embrace –
But am still stunned by the masterpiece of art that is your intricately carved form.
Each fingertip, each toenail, every detail is meticulously in its place
Every musculature perfect, up to the toned curves of hips and ass
That look so sculpted I stand in awe at the power of the sculptor
To make you so stunning, so present… so perfect…
I examine each hair carefully curled above mound
Puffy with the petals slightly parted as I touch your intimate flesh
And gasp along with you as your statue animates
And I breathe in your beauty as you breathe in my wonder

And slick folds clasp questing fingers as I continue my wandering adventure
Warming skin replaces marble cold as statuesque beauty shudders in lusting need
As Master Sculptor gives breath of life simultaneously alongside me, her Adam's stare
You, my Eve; and We, two new souls cavorting along the Garden of our Eden.

Mutuality

And there's something about you.
Every time our souls touch, sparks fly.
The same way lust fires indecent kaleidoscopic fireworks lighting up my mind's sky –
You turn me on.
Your voice is like warm honey caressing my mental faculties
With this sexy lilt that melts me the same way butter melts under the warmth of your sunny disposition.
You feel so right
Like if you were always here, were always meant to be right here tucked gently under my loving gaze
As though we were always meant to be together but, somehow, we just got displaced
And our bodies manifested in different parts of the world.
Yet time doesn't matter.
Time nor space are not constraints to the power of the attraction we feel.
It's as though we are supposed to be together whether we are near each other or not
As though the concept of distance is artificial
For
When we touch our souls alight
Our bodies have yet to taste what our spirits already have experienced:
The glory of oneness, of togetherness

There's just something about you:
I can't articulate it though I am trying to string words together to hold my thoughts,
Even though I know what I'm weaving is a straw basket which leaks
And my thoughts drip out incessantly because I'm constantly thinking about new ways to be with you….
And the sexuality of our authenticity is undeniable
Unfathomable
Incredible
I want to be the holder of all your secrets
And, with my acceptance, scrub 'dirty' from your vocabulary
It's like just hearing your voice and our clothes fall off
As we stand naked and unashamed, basking in the light of each other's presence
There is a safety in our nakedness, a realness in our openness
For there is a knowing that you will not hurt me, nor I you…
For there's something about you….
There's just this thing alluring about you…
This thing magnetic about you
And I intend to explore you until we uncover you
And be explored until you uncover me
Until we merge into one beautiful melody
Of togetherness.

Foreplay (2)

I don't want to stop.
I want my words to grow stiff and hard and long,
And your ears to be wet and fluffy and pink.
I want each word to leak sexy precum as it plays along your olfactory canal.
I want to rub my word's head upon your ears' petals
And tap upon your inner ear's nub, causing you to moan
I want each word to make you beg me to enter you
As you want each phrase to stretch your mind just so – filled to capacity.
I want my words to fuck you until an inch of your life!
So, no, I don't want to stop!
I don't want to stop.
I want your mind to part its thighs and invite me in.
I want your dripping thoughts to pulsate in anticipation of the pounding you will get
When I start to whisper – my soft tone making mockery of the power of each syllable.
I want to feel your mind grip my words in Kegel-like exercises
And let your needs make every part of you flood in desire.
I want to bend closer,4th making sure each thrusting word gets deeper.
And as I speak, I feel your inner ear vibrate with the need of me.
I want to stroke you with my masterful sentences
I want to spread your mind wider and release all your inhibitions.
I want to command your mental orgasms

And I want to see your body follow suit.
I don't want to stop!
I want your body to drip with every sound I make
And, when I finally slip finger into weeping crevice,
I want to smile, knowing my seduction is complete.

Tasting The Glory

I want to taste the Glory of your Femininity
I'm ready to pray to the power of the Divinity
Between spread legs.
I kneel at the entrance to the Temple
And breathe ....
Ready to take my Holy Sacrament
My Communion...
I Cum to the union of lips on lips
Pink lips upon pink slit
And sip ....
Drinking deep from Womanly chalice
The wine in your waist as hips grind and move
Around and around as joy abounds
And feasting upon your fleshy mound
Incense rising heady from between your thighs
Making both worshipper and worshipped high
Off the power of your exaltation
Beads of excitation spill from chalice lips
And I eagerly lick... them ... up....
And taste heaven!
I see stars!
For I taste the Glory and the power of the God (dess)
As I worship on my knees under raised dress
I close my eyes .... and am transported instantly to Paradise
Drinking the *amirita*.... the ambrosia...

The Nectar of the Gods
And I am no longer just a piece of flesh
I have mated with Divinity
And have, myself, become Divine
Transformed by the Holy of Holies
Instantly
Forever ruining me for the
Mediocrity of the ordinary
For ... once I tasted God ...
No normal food will do!

Instantly Wet

She said I wrote things that made her instantly wet,
And my smile could rival the sun's –
For I imagined my words making her womanhood tingle
With the dexterity of guitar fingers plucking her g-strings,
And imagined me whispering probing poems
Pushing past cotton barriers to flood her insides with desire,
Involuntarily moistening her gusset with my thrusting syllables.
Oh! She loves when I write things that make her instantly wet…
Like when I describe the way my tongue chases her implosion with circular strokes
Making feminine nature stand at attention, peeking from beneath hooded restraint
And matching the pinkness of her sodden thong
That melts under the intensity of my poetry.
I want to make her instantly wet
So I craft my words to match the vibration of my voice
That spells "Hitatchi" with every hum of my baritone
Making her press into me with the craving need to release
And, when she does, feel her flood both her mind and her thighs with my scribe
Instantaneously.
She said I wrote things that made her instantly wet,
And my smile could rival the sun's –
For I imagined my words making her womanhood tingle
With the dexterity of guitar fingers plucking her g-strings.

Open Up

Open up…
Let me see the beauty of your femininity
As shyness parts along with thighs;
Let courage shine as slit glistens in the light of my adoration.
Open up…
Let me taste the passion of your lips,
As my nature rises with the anticipation of our joining.
Let my desire to worship at your pearly gate.
Make my every move slow, purposeful, reverential:
Feel my fingertips grace the skin along your inner thigh,
Feel the sigh rise from sensitive skin as goosebumps follow my caress,
Feel the breath of my heated need hover – just so – right above your entrance,
And open … wider….
Let me enter with questing finger, dipping beneath the surface.
Let shyness fall aside with composure
As questing finger searches deeper,
Seeking the elusive button, the ridge of pleasure hidden from view –
Except for the truly worthy.
Open up…
Feel fingers curling in serene worship,
Finding tender spot upon upper wall's quivering flesh,
And may the call to cum hither start slowly, deliberately,

As excitement simmers.
Temperature rises.
Open up ….
Lips above, as below, part in silent scream;
Pressure built up until valve releases.
Eyes squeezed shut, and voice breaks silently,
Above the threshold of human comprehension.
And, suddenly, the call the cum hither, comes thither….
Liquid elation flushes down willing probing digit,
Flooding skin with scent of musky jubilation,
And screams, muffled by over-stimulation, find volume
Moans and shudders given voice as body shakes, as lust liquefies.
I close my eyes, aural fixation satisfied,
As I slowly remove my finger from the depths of your soul,
And kiss your upper lips, preparing for the trip down
To the dripping south.

Muse

Holding you was heaven and I pretended to be an angel with a devilish streak,
Kissing gently on cheek when I wanted to seek the back of your throat.
Wanted to trace my tongue down naked skin,
Painting hieroglyphics in infinity symbols, making desires known…
My art meeting your heart as my words pierce eager mind;
Sublime twists of tongue and rhyme causing panties to beat in time
With the throbbing of your … need.
Let me feed your desires for more than PG-13 thoughts
As my words twist and turn like your hips ought to be doing –
As my mind cavorts in ecstasy navigating the curves of your femininity
With every metaphor and simile.
May my lust speak orations as your beauty inspires me to create
Driving the artist in me to drive stiff syllables onto page while imagining
That my pen is piercing past pleasure's protective palisade
Piercing you with my penile pondering
Wondering how beautiful you would look under me – writhing.
Be my muse
Not just in my fantasies, making my thoughts cavort in pleasure

But transcending realities; unravelling the mysteries of our carnalities
'Cause I'm sure you'll love it as much as I will
'Cause I'm tasting the touch of you, still
'Cause I'm craving the feeling of filling you
Feeding you
Feeling you
And I stop …. Grow still … and reminisce…. 'cause….
Holding you was heaven and I pretended to be an angel with a devilish streak,
Kissing gently on cheek when I wanted to seek the back of your throat.
Wanted to trace my tongue down naked skin,
Painting hieroglyphics in infinity symbols, making desires known
Be my muse …. let my art manifest in every squeal, every moan.

Warmth

Warmth:
Slowly enveloping consciousness like
Comfortable feeling when you thaw out,
After sitting silently in a room warmer than the chill outside;
Eyes closing involuntarily.
Moan escaping lips as warmth slips over you
Like slipping under a downy comforter
While rain trickles down shivering window pane.
Slipping inside, feeling wetness coating skin
Moist warmth like the comfort of eating a freshly baked cookie
Crumbling under the intensity of ravenous carnality
That disintegrates resolve with every thrust.
Wet heat cradles
Lubricating piston translating twisting latent sensual energy
To kinetic
Rhythmic
Basic physic lessons – or, should I say, alchemy,
Because matter is transmuted to other elements in the blink of an
I
Or, rather, a 'We'
Because there is no I in the fact that it takes two to tango
And we roll hips simultaneously with the power of our feelings
And the warmth of your femininity raised like an oven to above melting point
And our mutual need melts under your fire

Until boiling point is surpassed
And orgasmic explosions decimate our combined essence.

Delicious

And I call you Delicious
As your legs part and I see your inner beauty
I call you Delicious
As your chocolate thighs mesmerise me and tempt me to taste
I call you Delicious
As your feminine folds make me lose all sense of time
I call you Delicious
As I focus on your curves that make my pen move and my thoughts rhyme
I call you Delicious
Oh! I want to trace your lips with my stiffened pink muscle
And I call you Delicious
Want to explore the depths of your soul as I prepare to consume
And I call you Delicious
Your body is my Temple, and I am your willing Disciple
For I call you Delicious
I kneel, preparing myself to take my Holy Sacrament
And I need your Delicious
As my lips trace your lips and I call you Divine
I praise you, Delicious
As you pulse in need, my thrusting tongue beats in time
And I seek you: Delicious
As I close my eyes, focusing only on your pleasure
As I seek your Delicious

Ah! There it is! Your amirita, your ambrosia – the food of the Gods
And I taste your Delicious
Tasting the glory of your femininity, ingesting the beauty before me
And I taste heaven: Delicious!

Inspired

And I'm ready baby…
As ready as your hardened nipples standing stiff with anticipation,
Ready to be drawn into the wetness that is my salvation – my salivating need.
I'm ready to cup those twin bountiful blessings in both hands and suckle –
As though regressed to infanthood, drawing sustenance from darkened teat,
Bringing sweet release from suction, drawing soul's essence from my tongue's travels:
Circling around and around until I could describe your breasts as diamond-tipped;
Until moans slip unabated from slacking lips and eyes close tight,
Trying desperately to hold … them … back …
But failing miserably.
And I'm ready ….
Ready to slide my tongue lower, ever lower
Encircling your belly button, seeking weeping flower
Which, for now, is encased in black lace …
So, I trace the indentation of your feminine lips with my masculine ones
Embracing the scent of your lust rising like incense from hidden temple,
And I get ready to pray.

Mouth open, tongue seeking source of holy water
As lace is expertly pulled asunder, revealing the Holiest of the Holy lands
And my tongue is born again – being baptised once, twice, three times –
Hymns of longing rise like incantations, forming writhing prayers from fluttering tongue
And hips undulate in unison, following the song of the seduced.
And I'm ready, with head bowed in reverence
To move lips and tongue ecstatically across your skin, scribbling sacred script
Capturing the Holy writ upon every curve of your femininity
Celebrating your Divinity
Constantly dipping tongue tip into the wetness of your centre
Signing my name: I may be the writer – but I was Divinely inspired.

Magic

I now believe in magic….
As clothes disappear with a practiced wave of fingers,
And tongue meets skin, conjuring spells of wonder upon naked flesh,
I lay, enraptured, as incantations make goosebumps appear unbidden.
You, the conjurer of my dreams, inspire spells of excitation
As runes of power are drawn over and over upon my stiffening shaft.
My senses fly with the accuracy of hexes,
Soul exiting body with the wail of the overcome
And, as your wetness envelops my hardness, my eyes roll back in rapture;
Your sorcery my undoing, my darkness unravelling under your light.
Hips gyrate
In hieroglyphic patterns; lips form enchantments to release me from prison.
And I am free! Chains that bound for aeons shattered in an instant;
Dark shadows, whispering curses to entrapped ears, flee under the onslaught of truth.
You, the erotic emancipator, my sensual sorceress, freeing my soul from bondage,

Bringing me up from the depths of my self-imposed imprisonment to others' opinions
Until I see myself as you see me: purely, with no restrictions to our intentions.
You let things happen organically, like a druid celebrating nature's course,
And we, magicians in tandem, twisting trances upon trembling sheets
Cast amorous spells in dual worlds until parallel universes collide.
Away, foul doubts! Only faith remains …
Fear banished from the realm by Goddess decree
And alchemy performed with every twist of hip and heave of breast
Transmuting my pain into golden strands of confidence.
Magic is real…

Sensual Lullaby

Moan for me
Boiling emotions bubbling over the tip of my glans
Spilling in drops of precum down my shaft
My excitement matches your intensity
Moan For me
Make my breath ragged as desire rages
Hotter than molten magma spewing from split earth
You are making love passionately with every
Moan for me
Every sultry sound rolling like raging ocean
Whipped into frenzy with the naked need goading my body's tide
Making reason careen dangerously towards destruction
Smashing against the serrated teeth of seduction
That breaks your voice into a thousand slivers
Moan for me
Make me rock hard as body shakes to fight the desire to lose control
To forget propriety
And bury every inch of broken willpower repeatedly
Into your gripping femininity
Until the passion swelling from my hearing you
Moan for me
Explodes within you and coats your walls with the stickiness
Of my failed attempt to glue my self-discipline back together
Which, if I'm honest, I knew was impossible

The moment your voice broke
Along with my resolve.

Emotional Voyeurism

Open your heart like you open your legs.
Let me peek at your vulnerabilities,
Slyly seek secrets under insecurities and
Spy the core of you...
The real you, hidden like your skirt suit
Hides your nakedness. I confess that
Seeing under your sins turns me on
And that you feel secure enough around me to
Spread your modesty wide, showing the pink inside of your
Blushing indiscretions, makes me melt.
Open your heart wide, spread your mysteries' thighs
And let me see the wetness of your hidden anxieties:
Your fears of being judged, that I won't want to associate with you
After you raise your skirts and let me view your authenticity…
But - nothing would be farther from the truth.
See, that you trust me makes me feel humbled, grateful, filled unconsciously
With wonder and awe at your bravery for surviving as you did
And, though you hid your indiscretions, showing them now for public scrutiny
Is another act of bravery that endears you indelibly to me.
The act of honesty is an aphrodisiac, I am drawn to you even more than before.

I want to pull you close and protect you from the harshness of the world
I want to be your King, your Lover, your Daddy, your Protector
I want to shield you from pain, heal your heart and bring again that beautiful smile
That brightens the atmosphere when my own day is overcast with scattered showers.
So, don't take me to be too forward when I encourage you to strip for me.
Drop every fear, every indecision, every insecurity
And let them fall like the layers of your clothing dropping on our floor.
Stand naked before me, not just without clothes, but without your walls –
Truly vulnerable –
And let me reward your bravery with my security
Stiffened resolve penetrating again and again to the depths of We Rhythmically
Until we shatter into a million pieces of kaleidoscopic bliss
Rising again together to kiss away your fears, wipe away all your tears
And wrap you in my arms so you again feel safe.

Receptivity

For what we are about to receive
May the Lord make us truly thankful.
And we ... ARE thankful!
As lip slowly slips across slit
Dipping into the wetness that is Goddess Chalice,
I bow to taste Her goodness; Her *amirata* –
Ambrosia sweetly sliding down gullet
As I take the Holy Sacrament of You
Raising Chalice reverentially
Taking You into Me
Effortlessly.
With my tongue I trace runes across Your clit,
Making magic with figure eight hieroglyphics
As I invoke the power of the building orgasm.
I mutter incantations as I pull Your bud gently with my teeth,
Sucking eagerly until hips roll hypnotically upon our sheets,
Which themselves are blessed with Your wetness;
Holy Water sprinkled liberally from Yoni
Until We both are baptised,
Rising again in the Glory of the Goddess.

And then, we switch.

Standing strong, My rod of Power within your grasp
You gasp at how thick He stands, awaiting your attention.

And then it is Your turn to give reverence
As knees hit floor in worship of the God
Rigid member flexes
As pink tongue graces His tip
And He slips just so down waiting wet walls
Even as You cup my sacred sacs within your palms.
I moan as You lick my Rod with eagerness
Stiffness your pleasure, making You want to experience more
We soar above the clouds as You suck My staff
Making My hips buck in ecstasy
Rainbows exploding energetically behind closed lids.
And I …
I …. I start to lose my grip on this physical plane
And fly
As you hum and croon lullabies upon my length
Sucking the strength from my body
As my soul detaches
Floating between this realm and the next
With Your lips my portal,
We see the face of Divinity
As I release my sweetness down waiting throat.

Telepathy

Let me spread your cerebral cortex slowly and dick you down with
Thrusting thoughts that grow stiff –
Hard like granite –
At the anticipation of entering you,
Filling your mind with my words,
Where your mental walls stretch with the fullness of my thickened contemplations.
Our telepathic connection is strong – mindfucking with no hands, nothing tangible,
But mental gymnastics bending you over with ease
Testing cranial labia for moisture with penetrating phrases.
Mmmmmm … your mind is wet…
So let me tease you a little more.
I want you gushing
As our intellectual intercourse goes deeper with each roll of orator's tongue:
Going down inside your perceptions,
Making you cream with my ministrations,
Sharing mutual intentions with the fluidity of lovers changing positions.
Let us share mental images that would make a psychiatrist blush
Until we can't take any more teasing
And I must get inside you
As my mind strokes yours from the back

And our connection grows stronger as synapses fuse
As our conversation continues, building in intensity…
Slowly at first, but then quickly building up some speed,
'Til the need to climax becomes overpowering
Sweat dripping off flexing mental muscle
Resisting the release… Straining … not wanting the connection to be severed
Until – there is no more waiting –
And spermazoaic sentiments spurt from stiffened reason
Into mind opened by prolonged deliberating.
Now … for the gestation….

Temptation

Eyes slowly slide sensually down smooth silky skin;
Fingers trace figure eights as you entice me, begging me to come closer.
I want to touch you, want to make my sensual dreams lucid.
You are bringing me to the brink of letting go –
To the edge of reason,
To the precipice of pleasure,
And then slowly withdrawing your attention, playing with me.
Repeatedly.
You are my Temptress…
I see the rise and fall of bounteous breasts, begging me to bring
My bite to bear on bared flesh,
Wanting to feel the folds of feminine rolls firm within my grasp.
You always think you're imperfect because you are not flimsy to the touch,
But don't you know it is your formidable form that makes me lust late into the night?
I want to trace teasing touches towards your treasure,
Yet deliberately skipping the pleasure of parting your nether lips with my tongue,
Teasing you as you tease me, bringing the temptation ever closer….
But this is all still within my future plans as you will not come close enough for me to hold.
You keep teasing me. Tempting me.

Go on. Keep doing it. Because when I get my hands on you,
My lips on you …
My hips on you …
When I get my revenge on you, just know that it will not be served cold,
But the tempting you exert on a brother will be repeated and increased ten-fold
Until your body craves the release you refuse to relinquish upon me.
And then I will continuously tempt you unto the brink of reason
Teasing until your treasonous body betrays you
And until your convulsing cavern quakes with the repressed energy finally getting release
Upon eager fingers
Seeking the elusive ball of nerves playing ecstasy in the key of G.
See – I have plans for you, so you can keep tempting…
Just know that when the roles in this game are finally reversed –
You will finally fully know the true definition of Temptation.

Morning Fragrance

I love the scent of flowers in the morning....
Petals unfurling as legs are a-parting;
You smile, and my eyes light up with the revealing,
Smattering of curls gleaming in the naughtiness of your wink!

Oh! I love the scent of flowers in the morning....
Nose parting dark leaves, tongue salivating in the anticipating;
Desire rising like incense from between sweet slit, emanating
And I am in worship, prostrating before the Holiness of spread thighs!

I love the scent of flowers in the morning...
Staff vibrating, my need stiff, resonating;
I grip myself, willing myself to control myself: concentrating,
As I bow my head in reverence, tasting the Nectar of the Gods!

I love the scent of flowers in the morning...
Tongue flicking weeping slit, my eyes closed, marinating;
I am raptured from the earthly plane to the Heavens, transporting,
All because of sexy yoni, wetness gleaming in softness of the Light!

Dark Sugar

Melininated molasses melted over sinful curves,
Complimenting resplendence of stunning smile.
I lick my lips, causing excited saliva to seep into eager mouth
Wanting desperately to eat – and not just with my eyes.
Your beauty arrests me, makes me stir your dark sugar with Hershey's kisses
That trace a trail from slender neck to chocolate drop areolas with pink lips,
Sipping sweetness as nipples pebble; sugar addiction making me suck just
A little bit harder….
Soliciting soft moans as molten heat mellows with the suction.
Chocolate mounds of beauty push deeper into waiting mouth
And hands trace sugar trails down sweet curves to wide hips,
Spreading Oreo thighs so I could get to the creamy treasure inside.
Fingers slip into the wetness of sticky sugar sauce,
Where my x marks the v spot, making her see spots
And making *the* spot moist with anticipation.
I taste your excitement upon dripping fingers
Which does nothing to sate my thirst for you…
In fact, it inflames it – makes it impossible to hold on to my restraint any longer:
My hunger grows stronger, and my lust stretches longer
To reach from my tongue into your sweet spot making me ponder the meaning of life,
When my lips meet yours, coating my face in your essence

Like a pastry chef coating the surface of a chocolate cake with frosting
And I am lost in … ecstasy… licking for all I am worth…
Tasting the centre of your being;
The sweetness once hidden now revealing to my questing tongue.
My hands spread your thighs, eyes closed, and I am in heaven
As I swirl seven different ways at your pearly gate
Making heads and eyes roll with the overpowering sensations.
Your moans my motivation to introduce my own sugar stick
Thick and chocolate rod teasing your sugar entrance
Introducing it entrances, making sweetness overpowering.
As movements marry to merge sweet syrup with whipped cream,
I scream into the nape of neck as stirring causes building tensions
More rhythmic sensations that build the intentions to increase gyrations to overpowering,
Deflowering complete, our mutual movements slow
Lips find upper lips as tongue slips inside a different set of pink
And as sugar stick sinks deeper into sugar walls
My body's incessant calls for dark sugar to sate my addiction are easing
Until my craving starts up again,
The teasing starts up again,
The needing starts up again
And I seek again after your melininated molasses melted over sinful curves
Seeking again my dark sugar fix!

Pink Poetry

Let me trace the inner folds of your pink with my poetry,
Let my curved consonants reach up – just so – and caress your clitoris poetically.
Let my elongated letters press deep into you, making you cream along their length.
My words are thick, and wide, filling your mind with a solid girth,
Encouraging a moan of pleasure as you feel completely full with the meatiness of my metaphors.
Let me give you something to grind on: imagery with ridges, similes with substance,
Making your mind gyrate as you contemplate the sexiness of my sentence structure;
Tracing the length of my lines with your questing, eager tongue.
Sucking the tip of my stanzas, making my phrasing bead with anticipation's precum
As we frolic in the abandon of our twisting, lustful thoughts…
Let me pull back the pink lace of your pink panty and expose the pink flesh of your womanhood
By whispering pink words against pink fabric to make pink wetness leak.
Let my baritone caress your curves, adding pink staccato spoken word to your pink secret places
And making curvaceous hips rock against the pinkness of my lips
As I use my pink tongue for more than just speaking.

I will be peeking into your sweetness with my pinkness – your taste is my weakness…

And then introducing my hardness to your wetness … with the quickness…

As my solid rhymes thrust into you in double time until your legs are shaking

Let me whisper pink poetry to your pink folds to make your pink walls pulsate

To make your lips flush pink with desire, swelling with the needing to be pummelled by penile prose,

Bringing both mental and physical up from the level of the lyrical to the literal

And making screams of pleasure our one and only goal.

Playtime

Tongues pulling to and fro
Tug of war
Battling to see which of us
Dominates
This playground.

Hide and seek
Sleek slick peck on cheeks
When I catch you...
(which ones do I really mean, though?)

So...
Meet me by the (sex) swings
For a rocking
Thrusting
Good time
Let's see how high we can go...

Spin the bottle
And wherever it lands...
Kiss
Long and hard
Will there be a clandestine feel copped in secret?
Squeezing her ass so no one can see...
Stealing into shadows

Wanting to explore…
Not for other's eyes
But for us to hear
The long low moan of pleasure
As I see how far my fingers
Can travel up your dress…

"I'll show you mine
if you show me yours.…"

Tingles
Wiggles
Trying to keep quiet
So we don't get discovered…
But exploration gets the better of us

And joy flows down
Coating fingers
Under pink cotton
Sinking deep

Cum with me
Cum for me

Don't you just love playtime?

Morning Conversation

Eyes rolling back as head thrown
Locs flown hither, thither, yon
As words flow over clitoris
With the power of Hitachi
Accent strokes baritone over ears
Air stained with the scent of Caribbean's rhythm
Intonation's penetration
Humming in appreciation of the lovely sound
Of
"Cum …. Cum … Cum for me…."
The sound of restraint cracking
Breaking under the undulating of hips
Tip of toy teasing tongue trembling
No – not that tongue….
Not those lips….
But the petals are in full bloom
Under the influence of the stream of our words.
As I always say
"Wordplay is my foreplay"
Well, today it held true
As I watched you feel my words grow thick
And long
And stiff
And push deep into the recesses of your wetness
And … And … And…

Release….

Again…. And Again… and Again…

Till sheets were soaked with the evidence of your exhilaration

Until, embarrassed, you stripped your bed

And we laughed

And our easy energy flows from one topic to the next

Until we again meet in the middle

Making pink petals push open

To receive my words again

And then we have to force our energy to part

You to the bath

And I to start my day ….

"What a lovely day….

Lovely day

Lovely day

Lovely day

Lovely day…." (sung to Lovely Day by Kirk Franklyn)

Touched

You touch – softly:
Quivers of desire
Shooting through
Feminine folds,
With Creation
As Intention.
Incantations wail
With Passion's moans,
As fingers stroke the
Centre of your
Moisture.

You touch – softly,
Calling my name;
Envisioning barriers
To our togetherness
Falling like dominoes
Under the onslaught
Of your will.
Magicians hands touch
And weave spells with
Enchanted fingers,
Tracing runes of power
Around and around
Excited raised nub.

I feel your touch
As you cry out
To the Heavens
Roaring your birthing
As Creating brings forth
The ending of gestation
The spasms of new life
Bringing forth the beauty
Of realising what was
Purely imaginary
Into to physicality
Of the real.

I crave your touch –
Not just across the astral plane
But face to face
Touching flesh
Parting lips exposing pink
Sinking deep into your excitement
Until excitement explodes upon my fingers
And I celebrate your touch
By taking your liquid love upon my lips
And touching you again!

Alchemy

For me, alchemy is the transmutation of latent sexual energy into words,
Making me become a master manipulator of matter.
Since energy can neither be created or destroyed – only transformed,
I use my literary prowess to process the power of pleasure,
Professing my deepest desires.
'Cause, when sensuality becomes my canvas,
Words become the paint through which I colour all creation
Creating masterpieces, interpreting the sexuality around me
Into poetry to make your body tremble
With skillful manipulation of simile, metaphor and imagery…
Even a little hyperbole thrown in for good measure.
So, feed me the intimacy of your deepest thoughts
Let me peek under your vulnerability, exposing the secrets of your wetness
For I wield the power to bring life to your hidden side
Without making you feel ashamed to be a sensual being
For being the object of my devotion means that your emotions will be centre stage
And I will take the time to craft my thoughts of you into something exquisite.

Intentions

Let my words slide effortlessly between your folds.
Let my every phrase stroke you until you drip down my throat with abandon,
Lubricating every lustful thought to make more poetry spill from my lips into yours…
Until my yearning slips easily into your sugary canal
And you are filled to the brim with my hardened need
Causing you to cry out, drunk in pleasure….
Let me part your walls with metaphors, stroke deep with imagery
And play sexual symmetry with similes until your bubble bursts
Until restraint is cast to the four winds and until the good girl persona flees
Being left with the wantonness of primal yearnings churning!
Once far beneath the surface, my verse makes hidden jewel sparkle
As legs part of their own volition, begging probing fingers finish what naughty poet started!
I whisper my intention to your pulsing petals, making them quiver with desire,
Every syllable lighting a fire I plan to put out with poetic penetration.
Cum and spread thighs wide at the influence of my spoken word,
Let the rumble of my baritone be the vibration that makes lady parts tingle

With lashing tongue! May my words make love to your labia sweetly,
Speaking subtly to make inner core tremble incessantly until exploding
And my words drink your essence until my poetic flavour is tinged with the scent of you.
Let my voice's volume raise! Let words penetrate with increasing fervour…
Let the rhythm of my poetic tongue pierce your mind with pounding thrusts
That make your inner core beat in unison with my savage invasions!
Oh! Let your wetness contract around the hardness of my spoken word
As my repetition makes us climb ever higher towards elusive peak
Until, with shouts of victory, we reach the point of no return
And my words make your mind and body erupt in violent frenzy!
Screams of elation preface ejaculation
As my words shoot multiple orgasms into the far reaches of your consciousness
And body mimics mind as wetness floods your thighs…
Skin flushed as you come down from the mountaintop
Sexually sated after being mentally penetrated!

Erotic Poetry

There's erotic poetry on her skin –
Pulling me in seductively,
Tantalising me till I can't resist the urge
To touch so gently, feeling the burn of electricity where
my fingers press softly into her melanin
And my skin sinks in to divinity –
For I have touched God – and my life would never be the same again.
Coz there's erotic poetry in her curves,
Sinuous symmetry of sensuality in every swishing line
My mind traces her suppleness, and when we kiss, sonnets spring forth,
Erupting overhead like fireworks
Synapses firing as fingers stroke her hair, her back, the curves of her ass….
And I am lost in the mystery of her beauty.
There's erotic poetry on her lips
While our bodies merge with the rhythm of spoken word stanzas
Lips meeting and parting and meeting and parting and meeting and…
Thrusting tongues convulsing as my pen is dipped inside her ink
Sinking deep with every roll of hips writing in cursive upon the pink pages of her lust
Our bedroom an open mic for two
Moving metaphors make melodies merge as moans meld together

Making music together in the symphony of sex…
There's erotic poetry on your skin:
Let us start a movement!

Waiting

Your eyes meet mine …
And lock –
Time stands still as
Lovers copulate with combined gaze:
Trysts shared with single stare -
Lust evident.
Silence grows;
The anticipation.
Then …
Thighs part as if by magic,
Trimmed treasure glistens in dim romantic light.
Your invitation causes my excitation.
Wetness of arousal stains air with scent
As hardening resolve raises nature
And body positions itself for initial thrust.
I capture hardened nipple with eager lips
Prolonging the suspense,
Teasing you.
Hardness touches wetness gently
Stroking tip to slit…
Taunting…
Causing moans of frustration from
Eager feminine lips
Both sets weeping with the need for filling;
I'm praying – thanking the Universe for the Healing

Praying also for me staying in control –
Resisting the urge to release before the time! –
I am the master here;
I'm in control ….
I'm … waiting….

Thirst

Bend to my will
And take my rod
Deep inside your
Pulsing cavern
As you hold your ankles
Screaming for Daddy to
Push in deeper.
I thirst for you;
I want to feel you.
Hands grip hips possessively
Grunts meet moans
As thrusts bounce repeatedly
Against round globes of flesh
Trusting that
I know how to handle you
Making you submit
Sweat drips from skin
As we battle for dominance
I crave your submission
But you won't give it willingly
I exert my dominance
Cum-manding you on every turn
Every desire
My will your only consuming thought
Take these deep strokes

Let me make you melt
Give me everything you have
Everything you are
Satisfy my thirst!

Filthy

I'm sliding my tongue down your brain at the crease between hemispheres
Imagining I have you bent over, spread wide
Running that same muscle between the crack of your ass
My poetry is filthy tonight….
I want to tongue fuck your thoughts
As though you are getting me to consume your creamy lust from behind
Dripping with every thrusting syllable
And your thoughts are wet
With every word I speak your mind gets soaked
You are face down, ass up on my obscenities
Presenting your most intimate parts to my penetrating pen
Feeling every roll of my consonants
The rhythm of my stiffness pushing deeper than anyone's ever been
And you beg me to fuck you
You are spreading your mind like your ass cheeks
Begging me to defile you with every line
And I comply
My tongue slides down your brain at the crease between hemispheres
I have you bent over, spread wide,
As I mentally run my pink muscle up and down the crack of your ass

Mindfucking you mercilessly as I dominate every thought
Controlling your cum....
Releasing only when I say: at the end of my poem.
And as my oration ends, fingers replace words,
Testing for moisture
And getting ready for round two....

I Want a Hug

I want a hug.
A wet, warm, squeezing hug.
An ass-grabbing, loud moaning
Hip thrusting hug.
I want a debaucherous hug
A prowling, prancing, growling,
Bodies rolling hug;
A lip biting, breasts grabbing,
Animalistic hug.
I want an overpowering hug
That eclipses all others.
I want a nipple sucking hug,
A slow grinding hug,
A slushy hug;
I want a stirring mac and cheese sound kinda hug.
A queefing hug,
A wetness shooting across the room hug,
A screaming obscenities in passion
Kinda hug,
A wake the neighbours then
Passing out in exhaustion kinda hug
Fuck it….
I just need a hug….

Breakfast in Bed

Let my tongue
Find the
Sweetest syrup
Between spread legs;
Coating the juiciness
Of your exposed mango,
Getting ready to
Help me satisfy
My daily nutritional
Requirements.
Feed me your chocolate-
Covered strawberry
And may the doctor be
Kept away
When I take my daily
Dose of your apple
Shaped mounds.
Let me not be selfish:
Let me feed you the
Stiffness of my
Sausage,
Making sure you get
Your fill
Of a sensual
Smoothie.

We take turns having
Breakfast in bed
Until we can't eat anymore
Until we are both
Satisfied!

Pied Piper

I am the Pied Piper of Pleasure:
My beginning stanzas start to enchant you, moistening your lips
As though they lick themselves in anticipation of the sweetness to cum,
And by the time I'm done, my ending leaves you pulsing and gushing,
Panting with the exertion of the explosion that your body has just overcome.
For I am the Pied Piper of Pleasure:
You do what I say, when I say and how I say – no hesitation, no question;
For I am the executive officer of your orgasms, your Cum-mander-in-Chief –
In short, I am your Sir.
So, get down and give me fifty push ins, as I push my poetry into your wet gushing mind
And your body follows in kind as you gyrate upon my spoken rhythms
And ejaculate expressions of rapture – wetting me with every moan and shiver
As I coax you to heights unimaginable with just the timbre of my voice.
I am the Pied Piper of Pleasure:
Making you touch yourself with the power of just my words
Let me hear you cum, but only ever at my cum-mand

As I make you understand that you don't own a single one – they manifest only when I say NOW!

Somehow, I continue to pull orgasms from your body like some lewd magician

Pulling rabbits from your twat and – just like that – your body is convulsing for the fourth time

Keeping time with my encouraging baritone.

I am the Pied Piper of Pleasure:

Are you willing to submit to receive joys multiplied beyond measure?

Are you able to give me your orgasms without reservation?

Are you ready to cum?

Let's go … ONE… TWO … THREE….

NOW!

Surprise

Legs spread inviting me to play
Smile leaves me speechless
And salivating
Clit winking "Cum play with me"
As cheeky fingers tease libido between wet folds
I want to play
But constrained by distance
Mind wandering between wet lips
Tasting the glory of your surprise
Mammary magnificence moves me
Heart beating rapidly
And yet stills me into silence
As I forget to breathe
Damn…..
Legs spread wide inviting me to play
Running up and down your body
In wild abandon
Replace your fingers with mine
Intertwine arms above your head
Holding them in place
As lips slowly take in all of your taste
Dine at your dinner table
Slowly sipping the wine slipping down throat
From slit most succulent
And smacking lips simultaneously

Supping until satisfied
Give me your sex until you shatter:
And legs close in ecstasy around bowed head.

Waiting

Your eyes meet mine ...

And lock –

Time stands still as

Lovers copulate with combined gaze:

Trysts shared with single stare -

Lust evident.

Silence grows;

The anticipation.

Then ...

Thighs part as if by magic,

Trimmed treasure glistens in dim romantic light.

Your invitation causes my excitation.

Wetness of arousal stains air with scent

As hardening resolve raises nature

And body positions itself for initial thrust.

I capture hardened nipple with eager lips

Prolonging the suspense,

Teasing you.

Hardness touches wetness gently

Stroking tip to slit...

Taunting...

Causing moans of frustration from

Eager feminine lips

Both sets weeping with the need for filling;

I'm praying – thanking the Universe for the Healing

Praying also for me staying in control –

Resisting the urge to release before the time! –

I am the master here;

I'm in control ….

I'm … waiting.…

Part 2:
PAIN

Call Me for Prayer

"Call me for prayer…"

Where?

Blasted on FB

Publicly

As tho' everyone should see how far I've fallen?

And I need help to get up

From who?

You?

Don't make me laugh!

Your rod and staff don't inspire confidence.

They bring out the beast in me

Make me snarl cruelly

Thinking how *easy* it would be

To wash you off in cuss words

Poetically…

I don't need the high and mighty

"Call me for prayer…"

I need the brother who will be there

When tears flood my face

Who isn't disgraced

To come alongside someone sitting in the dirt

And you wonder why I "flirt

With the world?"

'Cause there's more genuine love

Out here than under the pious stare

Of the righteous….

For real, don't make me cuss

'Cause all I've heard is how I'm throwing away my life

When all the while I'm battling loss

And when I need you, you gloss

Over my need and tell me

How I've fallen away?

Yet I remember the hugs

Surrounding me

when loss wracked my body

and no one offered to pray,

just allowed me to be;

not throwing jargon.

I'm sure that if I was next to Christ

He would comfort

Instead of consorting

Spitting religious verbosity

I know you mean well, see

But time and place would dictate

A privately penned message

Not a blast on my Timeline

For all to see

That you're 'helping' me

'Cause the same Christ you following

Said "Don't let your left hand see

What your right hand is doing…"

So, in my ruling,

You need to wheel and come again

Or rather – don't come back at all

'Cause I don't need to deal with all the emotion

You stir up; one simple message pulled up

And my day lost all its bearings

Like a doomed plane losing altitude

Veering to an explosive end.

I had to sit down and spend

The time to write this verse,

Expressing myself and saving you

From the curses rising unbridled to my lips

So save us both the bother and take a trip

Taking your, "Call me for prayer" with you…

Gambler

I feel like I help women heal – not for me, but for the next one.

I feel like they use my comfort as a stepping stone,

Rising above their pain to triumph,

And then, move on.

I feel like I'm being discarded, left right where I fall…

When they have successfully

Navigated their labyrinth of pain –

feel whole again –

and,

Just when I think they'll stay and grow… they let go….and,

I fall into the hands of another ….

"Brother" …

I always am "Friend" to them

I always am here for them

And I'm the one left holding the short end of the stick

The shortest straw…

The problem is

The luck of the draw is that the house always wins

And I, a gambler at love's roulette

Keep spinning, looking in vain

For the jackpot.

Homicide

Fingers tracing exit wounds, reflectively;

Memories instinctively retracing steps

Like an errant thief returning unerringly to the scene of their crime.

Heart beats, slowly, carefully….

Life returning to normal

But

Kevlar is worn under my dress shirt now

As nightmares of kickbacks and slugs piercing flesh

Are still fresh on my mind.

Pain may be phantom now, but no less real:

Emotional upheaval the aftershock from

The shock of being shot by friendly fire –

Bullets barely missing most vital organs

But leaving gaping holes where my trust should be

As I struggle to breathe with a collapsed lung.

And, as I am gasping out …

As I am bleeding out…

I seek to understand where the shot could have come from.

Now, in recovery, my pain has lessened.

Sutures of time and apology have tied burst capillaries together

To allow blood to flow along familiar relationship routes again,

But, ever so often, sharp pains remind of old war wounds

Whenever the weather changes,

And, my mood changes to reflect the chill of bitterness that flows freely outside…

And I have to choose to close the windows of my soul against the chill
Choosing instead to stay close to the warmth of heartwarming moments
That remind me that I'm still alive in order to feel that chill
But still…..
My fingers trace the imprint of bullet shaped words that nearly took my life
And I reflect upon the day my love was almost murdered.

Battle-Weary

I wear my pain like armour:
Protecting vital organs from Disappointment,
Stabbing and slashing –
A great big ogre bearing down on me with drawn broadsword,
Out for the kill, but webbed scar tissue is impenetrable,
Keeping feeble heart still beating, for the moment.

I wear my pain like armour:
Swearing none will again get close enough to use sharp Expectations
As a dagger to gut me, slicing my soft underbelly open,
Bleeding bright red Hopes and Dreams, staining the ground,
Being left to die.

I wear my pain like armour:
And, even though it's heavy, its medieval weight is necessary, familiar.
My heart needs the weight to feel secure;
Chainmail protecting vital organs, heavy unwieldy shield big enough to hide behind
Keeping Sanity from being run through with Doubt's spears.

I wear my pain like armour:
Life is Battle of the Bastards hopeless, before the Knights of the Vale
And I am Rickon forgetting to zig away from zagging arrows
Being cut down in the prime of existence,
Though he (I) have not really started living yet.

I wear my pain like armour:
And continue to stand. Once gleaming in the Sun, my pain is now battle-weary, but holding.
I am still fighting, while others have given their lives on this battlefield
Not a blade of grass untouched by the spilling of blood,
Yet, still I stand, still I fight – and I will conquer!

Mirage

Desert wailing in anguish, lashing out
wind squeeeeeeeeeeeeeeeeeeeeeealing like
angry toddler throwing tantrums ,
chucking clumps of sand about like toys
around deserted nursery.
Sun hides in shame behind dusty curtain;
sudden haze dims the gaze into the distance.
It is hard to breathe.
Sand tries to find permanent home in gut,
replacing air carrying oxygen to starving lungs.
Bent figure crouched, hiding from murderous wind's intent
to slice at exposed throat.
Eventually, tortured tantrum passes.
Wind dies down, billowing sand cloud settles.
Weary traveller left to live another day – or maybe not.
Psychotic heat takes over killer storm's shift; dehydration imminent.
Moisture flees before onslaught of cloying drought –
MUST ..... FIND.... WATER......
Every step, an eternity.
Suddenly, glint whispers seductive hope to arid tongue,
renewing strength, putting hammer to pain's blockade.
Every step brings faith for liquid deficiency's reprieve,
The taste of cool water driving force for pushing forward.
Relief washed away in optimism's cleansing steam
bubbling up from anticipation's source.

Each step a joy, fierce sun now no longer harsh,

Traveller now confident refreshment is steps away....

Renewed energy infuses tired limbs; traveller pushes to cool fiery throat.

But, cruel Fate's prank

deals death blow's punch line:

Hours of walking, no closer to intended goal.

On reaching the spot where oasis should be found,

Refreshing salvation non-existent; only dry, dusty ground.

Love was only a mirage.

Momentary Clarity

Sometimes I forget that I should not box myself in

Should not label myself

Because labels are so easy

You know, pull of the backing and stick them on just right

'poet', 'author', 'spoken word artist', 'editor' are the labels I have on my lapels right now

Those are the ones I chose

But they aren't the ones I had to live with

They aren't the ones I had to soak off....

'nerd', 'Urkel', 'Spidey', 'oh-my-God-how-can-you-see (out of those things?)

Those are the ones I grew up hearing

Like evil schoolmates bound me with cords of derision and stuck them on without my consent.

I forget that I don't have to live in the boxes created for me

So every poem has the same structure

And I agonise over not really *wanting* to learn every piece

Because knowing it by heart will make me connect with my audience better

I struggle between wanting to be the best spoken-word artist I can be

And just writing for the hell of it again, for the fun of it again

Sometimes the business of writing strips away the joy in writing

When I think money isn't coming and

When books aren't selling and

I need to dip into my business account again to put gas in the car.....

But then I get inspired to just let go of all my preconceived notions.

I am inspired to soak the labels off again

For a moment, to be free again

Until gravity sucks me down

And the muck of conformity and routine pollutes the sanctity of my mind space again

I thank God for those times where the skies clear

And I feel the sun on my skin.

Moving On

What can I say? Three weeks passed away
 in the blink of an eye,
Watching friendship's burning rubble die
 Into fading embers – I remember potential and possibility.
Torn heart stripped – laid bare – and whipped
Within an inch of life by twists of fate
Coiled ropes foiled attempts at soaring to the skies…
But then again, hot air always rises.
I guess she wanted to have all the prizes….
Little minds need to ridicule to feel better:
The little exercise that made you feel wetter
Is now over, my part-time lover…
We had our fun, but now it's time to part
As you started to make this much deeper than was meant to be
Seeking fulfilment, sensuality, you said you wanted to teach me
How to stand on my own feet, I learned to be discreet
As we sneaked past office workers for a peek
Of the good life; caused momentary pause
As feet left the ground as we twirled together –
But crashed as you flashed the inside of your will
And showed it sinister, wanting to control,
Restricting the expansion of my soul
To bend to your desires.
Time to release soul from tormenting fires
Of trying to conform to another's choices –

No more bending to other's voices

Might call me a wuss but I'm roaring with

The noises

Of someone throwing chains off

Standing up and starting to scoff

At the attempt to bind me:

I'm on a mission to find me

And to bring myself back from the dark lands

So go, I bear you no ill will –

I recognise that I don't have the skill

To be your puppet toy;

Will release your aura and release the cloying

Affect we had on each other –

You can sleep, no longer a bother

And I will continue to live without guilt

And no more tears spilt

Over milk running down the crevices of life.

Oooops!

Oooops, excuse me… your superficiality is showing!
Better close your lips! *Shhhhhhhhhhhh!*
I don't need to be knowing the colour of your bitter soul
Start pulling your Freudian slip back down from off your hips,
Coz with everything you're saying, you're just exposing more and more of your ass…umptions.
Stop flapping, letting us see all your business, coz you're not good with concealing
The wedgie caused by having your panties all in a bunch!
The problem is this – I already suspected your shallowness;
Your mistake was speaking, opening your mouth, and thus, effectively erasing all doubt.
But, before you mute, tell me … what exactly does an erotic poet look like?
You whisper behind hands that if my abs were flat and tight that I would be appealing;
That, based upon the type of words I'm spitting, my physique should resemble a Greek god –
Maybe, Adonis?
Well, I'm sorry that my looks don't rock your boat. Just know that every quote I drop
Is meant to lubricate your mental labia, to make *you* feel sexy… even, *juicy*….
So exterior appeal is not as important to me as it seems to be to you…
Beauty, to me, is an internal affair.
My words are meant to excite your soul, not just your body.
Don't get me wrong! I do want to make your body hum too,

I want every word I speak to strum sensual rhythms across your sex –
Voicing incantations that put bewitching hex upon your mind and make …
you… cum…
Making you dare to strip off sopping underwear for comfort's sake.
But if, for fuck's sake, you can't get wet because you can't set eyes upon a
bulging set of pecs,
Then … that isn't my problem … it's yours! I don't write for you, live for you or do
Three sets of sit-ups hoping you accept my pen, or my penis.
This is not a popularity contest! I've done too much growing,
Knowing that changing myself to please others just doesn't fucking work.
But, know that you might miss out on a trip around the world my tongue can take you on,
As tales of lust are spun with skill, until your entire body hums with the attention
I give to your secret places, as I place my pinkness deep inside your wetness….
But – ooops! Excuse me, your superficiality is showing….
You will go to your grave never knowing the type of loving you could get from this poet
All because the packaging does not meet society's ideal of beauty
Trust me … But tell me … Are you all you want to be, sexually?
Do you look at yourself and say, "Daaammmmmmn I'm fine?"
Do you? Do you?
Coz, I do …

Package

No one likes unfinished packages.

They like everything just so:

Neat bows that close

Around a perfect box

That locks the real me inside.

Wrapping paper in place;

Setting aside.

Waiting for the right one

To pick up the

Perfectly wrapped gift…

And swiftly

Unwrap it.

Well fuck it!

Who said I want to

be the one to teach

Preach

Reach the broken -

Touch the unspoken?

No one likes to

come alongside,

help build up -

It ain't easy!

It's back breaking work!

Construction

From inception

To completion

Takes commitment,

Patience,

False starts,

Some broken hearts

And the will to

Start again when

We hit a wall...

No one wants

An unfinished package....

But to the one

With the courage

To crack it -

The mystery

Of the broken me,

That is -

To that one is given

The honour

Of seeing me flourish

As I am nourished

With love's irrigation,

As I plot life's destination

To be my heart's GPS;

My navigation

From shy to secure

In my own skin

Promising

The beauty of

Solidity

A firm foundation

To build a nation on.

Is that one

You?

Reality or Fallacy?

So ... what's reality?

I've built my popularity on sensuality, sexuality

But every time I step on stage I proclaim that Passion isn't always sex

So ... it's time for a lesson in vulnerability.... Authenticity....

What really exists? Or is everything I believe a fallacy of half-hearted hopes

Holding on desperately for the truth to be revealed someday

In some way ...

Striving for authenticity but yet retreating into my fantasy every time I close my eyes

You're here, not there and I swear It'll be the most beautiful romance in the world...

But, what's real?

Coz I got into this because I thought someone truly saw ME

And I didn't have to cloak myself in invisibility

And be someone else...

But that might have been a fallacy

Coz – surprise! – you're not satisfied and I .... I ... I...

I have to let myself go .... Let myself be free

To hit it from the back aggressively coz that's what you're familiar with.

And the fantasy continues because I have to put on a show to make you happy

And .... But .... What if ... what if I always am this way?

Will you stay ..... or will you decide the other is better....

What's the reality?

Can I disrobe in actuality, or will my authenticity scare you?

Will you dare to handle it or will I have to constantly wear two hats...

I thought you truly saw ME – and, mostly, you do….

You see through my fears and I know you want me to be better … But …

What if I never live up to your standard?

What if I never ascend to the pinnacle of your expectations?

Will you wait impatiently for me to get it? And if I never do ….

Will … will you …. resign yourself to the fate you dealt yourself

Or will your inner self counsel your outer self to self-destruct?

Will the escape clause finally be put in motion – will you run?

Or, rather, stay still, because you really don't have to move

Everything is there – and that leaves me here digging clay soil

Preparing for a transplanting that might never happen.

I have not written this way in a long time – maybe it's time that I do

Because Passion isn't always sex, sometimes, I get vexed….

But sometimes sad too….

Because I stand, waiting for a hand that should fit mine

But I see it dissolve into the pixelated ether

And I grasp air.

Tactile

Name one thing you want in a partner.

Hmmm

The one thing I want.

The one thing I want?

The one thing *I* want?

The one thing I want in a partner is ....

Presence

I need your presence....

No, not 'presents... I don't need your gifts.

Let me rephrase this:

Let me present the facts

I need your presence

I need your essence

Mixed together with mine indivisibly

I need you AND me

I need US ... together ... physically

I don't need the farce of imaginary hands caressing heart

As I l stare longingly into space

And use fingers to trace

A face

That is not there.

I need your presence.

I need to feel you with my skin

Feel the thump-thump-thumping

Of heart racing under the influencing

Of synapses firing because you physically

Touch me.

Come on, touch me.

Feel me.

See. Me.

See me, dammit!

What the fuck do you want from me?

Can we continue the illusion of you and me

When WE are nothing more than the joining together

Of the construct of happiness – without the foundation of realism?

sigh

I guess not.

So, It's time for me to get off the roller coaster

Time to stop the carousel and get out of the amusement park

I guess I wore out the amusement part

There seems no end to this merry-go-round

My emotions have just been spun around

Dizzily falling to the ground when the world stopped turning

But my perceptions did not.

So .... what I'm saying is

I can't name one thing I want in a partner ....

I need a partner first.

Tears

Emotions trickle wetly down quivering cheeks

And drip off my chin, struggling in vain to be strong:

I hate this part.

Balance is key ... absence makes the heart grow fonder...

All these cute sayings fizzle into insignificance in the heat of separation;

It feels like my heart is breaking.

Like it's already shattered into irreparable pieces

And I am left with a dustpan and hand broom

Trying to sweep up the shards

So my feet are not punctured while I walk past this pain

Because life has to go on.

Right?

This 50 first dates kinda love

This reconnecting every time kinda love

This strengthening our resolve kinda love

I take each breath because I must,

Breathing because by living I survive.

The pain is intense for a moment

Dulling to an ache that never really goes away

Until you are here with me once more.

So I hold it in, smiles shining through the tears

As I reminisce over memories nestled into our shared consciousness.

And I honour your role in my life in making me grow

Your influence, the light to my seed

Buried in the soil of potential

Germinating finally into new life.

So, as emotions trickle wetly down my quivering cheeks

And drip off my chin, as I struggle to be strong…

I give thanks

For you.

For you

You are the reason for my strength

You are the power behind my pen

You are the light shining from my eyes

And the motivation for my forward motion.

I am because you are.

And though we physically part

Know my heart stretches towards you from this you-niverse to the next

And back again.

We are never alone.

I love you.

Tempered Glass

Walk carefully – you have my heart.

You have the reason for my existence

Nestled within your arms, so don't drop her.

You have the connection to my soul:

The yin to my yang, the exhale to my inhale,

The two halves that made one whole,

As though we were learning fractions all over again.

The fractures of my heart were healed by her touch,

Her laugh is my medicine; her smile, the balm

That makes all things new again.

So be careful with her,

Because, although strong, she can still shatter.

Tempered glass can still fracture under enough pressure,

And I can't bear to see her crumble under the weight of disappointment.

So – walk slow – protect her.

Be the broad shoulder for her to lean on in my absence;

I entrust my heart to your oath of allegiance.

Treat her like the Queen of Sheba that she is:

The Ma'at that gives balance,

The Cleopatra that rules the River Nile,

For she is my Head of State, the monarchy of my society;

The one that surely claims the majority vote when elections come,

For all other contenders fall away and she does not even need to canvass,

But is ushered into office unopposed for another term.

So, walk carefully – you have my heart.

You have the reason for my existence

Nestled within your arms, so don't drop her.

The Fight

Emotions caught in dry throat – I can't swallow.

Heart hurts as expectations meet reality

With the finality of wrestlers hitting mat

And referee starts the countdown

10 … 9 … 8 ….

As I am pinned – do I struggle to get free, or just give up?

I can feel every blood cell traversing my arteries.

Body appearing normal, but imperceptibly, my nerves are shaking

Shivering under the onslaught of the mental blows I've been taking

And I sink into the mat, willing myself to get up…

But still unmoving….

And the referee continues counting

7 … 6 … 5 ….

Slowly, my head starts clearing from the ringing in my inner ear

Tinnitus starts to fade

Resolve rebuilding – I will not give in to the onslaught of my emotions

And I start shaking

Making my hurts fly off like water droplets flying from wet fur

Not faking my strength, but standing in it

Claiming it

As my mental fortitude is returning

The referee was still counting

4 … 3 … 2…

But there will not be a TKO tonight

I have arisen again to continue the fight

Battered and bruised, but I will not be defeated

At the end of the day

The referee will stop counting…

Because I will have

WON.

The Wind of a Thousand Whispers

Listen. You hear it? Be still. You feel it?

There it is again. And again.

Zephyr of confession rustling leaves of indifference.

Rustling discontent sending unease through societal atmosphere

Centuries of pain unearthed, hidden pain cracked as Pandora's box was found…

And opened…

Wind picking up speed.

There it is again….

Breeze blowing harder as courage formed in multiple voices

Those whose fear had kept them silent for too long emboldened by the disturbance in the atmosphere –

There is strength in numbers.

Whispers pick up pace.

Wind increases.

Whispers strengthen resolve as

Hardened patriarchal boughs sway wildly in the gathering onslaught

Whispers pick up gale force as t(r)opical depression gives way to international awareness

As multiple whispers reach hurricane force

There it is again … louder ….. faster …. Harder….

Collective whispers now uncontrollable … unstoppable ….

Snapping hardened hearts like twigs breaking off societal apathy

Lethargy and silence deafening

Silent too long … but no more!

There is no "I" in this storm….

Collective rage overpowers years of keeping the pot covered

To stay 'respectable' and quiet

To protect fragile masculine egos, fearful of Patriarchal backlash.

"Tell no one or I will kill you ..." "Let this be our little secret" "No one has to know...."

NO! NO MORE!

Whispers no longer! The murmur of individuals tsunami strong

WE WILL NOT BE SILENT!

In the face of trepidation, we will speak our truths

Where will the wind of a thousand whispers take us?

What will the voices of a million women make us?

Women standing – defending – ripping the scab off societal ugliness for all to see

Coz see... the society's infected ... sickness pervasive

So invasive that – just like the other big C – it ate away at cells undetected

But this cancer is not cervical – it's callousness

And needs radical corrective consciousness to be corrected

Subjected to aeons of abuse at the hands of those they respected

They have finally objected – and as the movement gathers momentum

This hurricane will devastate

Intimidate

Frustrate

Complicate

Those whose skins are thinner than paper

But I beg to differ! I pray, do not waver

Coz Passion is more than sex

And I know that the wind of a thousand whispers

Will bring forth change.

Vigil (1)

Candle lit

Life extinguished

Errant bullet

Erasing potential in an instant.

Family in turmoil

Upheaval of societal bile vomits

At the stench

"Something is rotten in the state…"

As dem mark another one to die

As the motto

"To serve and protect"

Gets trampled.

Who is protecting now?

Another ascends to ancestor prematurely

Selwyn's spirit rises to clasp hands with I'Akobi

And solemnly

Now we march

Holding candles

Commemorating life

Mourning

Weeping

Wondering

Standing

Demanding justice

As we

Keep vigil

And

Ancestors rise

Acknowledging his entrance.

Vigil (2)

I stand, screaming, as expectations die

Crucified on elevated planes;

What was cannot now be.

"Eli, Eli, lama sabachthani?"

Is this the end of the era of happiness that engulfed us?

We - swept away in Passion's tide -

Now crushed

Wave of euphoria crashing upon reality's shore

Vainly surfing climax's crumbling crest…

But, everything has changed.

Can visions of peace still be seen

While carnage greets the naked eye?

Can a day where no one dies be imagined

While cadavers are carted away

And the stench of death hovers?

The Grim Reaper's scythe is busy…

Kryptonite

Strength bleeds as resolve crumbles

Self-determination fades

Thoughts of you assassinate composure

And, though, invulnerability is highest when apart

Proximity makes knees weak.

Resolutions to let you go melt under need's onslaught:

Respecting decisions, keeping feet planted forward,

Letting you follow path of light –

All melt under the molten gaze of Passion's trigger.

I think about your smile

And I forget my promises

I want you back.

Morning Thoughts

Is it wise to let you deep inside again?

Wise to open old wounds, just because I don't want to be alone?

Can I trust you not to hurt me?

Are you going to play me? Use my good nature to get what you want

Then string me along like a fool

Dangling promises

And I, the jackass,

Straining for the carrot that is just out of reach?

Is it wise to let you deep inside again?

True, I am not the scared broken one you met before…

But the Lion's mane still frames a gentle heart

And I don't want to be broken

Upon the altar of culpability

Lord let me know ….

I still have my self-respect.

Persona Non Grata

I guess that's what I am now: persona non grata

Formless

Shapeless

Nothingness

Non-existent.

Can I find peace in the childishness now?

For you are still chained to your grudges like the proverbial ball and chain,

But it never kept you restrained! Maybe that fear weighed me down instead,

Because for far too long I had to feel the grip of fear whenever our paths crossed.

I was trying desperately to be perfect:

Perfect employee with perfect attitude and perfect attendance –

But no one is perfect all the time

And pressure to be perfect at all times made me stutter

Stumble over crossed lines as communication sputtered

And not understanding your wishes made 'mistakes' occur –

Even though I felt they were more missed takes on your requests:

Take 1 – "I want this report…"

Take 2 – "This is not what I asked for…"

Take 3 – "I have to always check back behind you…"

Take 4 – "Listen, just let me do this myself…."

And I always say I take my licks – but sticks and stones may break my bones

But words – they devastate me…

Or, at least, they used to…

For it's not to say I'm not trying, but how can I assist correctly when your explanations
Of what you want leave me wanting? I mean, I'm not trying to find fault in your logic –
But sometimes what you say you want and what you actually want keep defaulting
To *Error* *Error* *Syntax Error* *Unable to compute…*

The edge of contempt in your voice slices through composure like a brand-new scalpel,
My scalp pulled into the beginnings of a migraine from worrying if I would get yet another thing wrong;
I'm stressing 'cause I'm trying to adhere to every desire,
Yet the fire of determination burns my own skin under the glare of your disgust.

So now I am persona non grata

Formless
Shapeless
Nothingness
Non-existent.

I speak and you ignore my greetings – even as fleeting as they are, I still try to show manners

But my words fade into the ether as though I'd never spoken. Okay – I hear your silence loud and clear

My fear hardens into hard, cold metal. Okay, this game is mental …

And I will out-manoeuvre you until I put you in checkmate.

I will win this fight.

I have always been a creative working in a logical environment –

A fish walking on land, having learned to breathe air

But always I crave the smoothness of the rolling sea

I seek the inspiration of the waves.

For even if I am persona non grata:

Formless

Shapeless

Nothingness

Non-existent.

I will not let your ignorance nullify my existence.

About the Author

Robert R.Gibson (**PassionPoet**,or **Passion**, for short) enjoys painting sensual images with his words, leading his audience into a sensory experience. Although sexuality and sensuality are his main forte, in his own words he says, "Passion is not always about sex." Passion is anger, sorrow, enthusiasm - his poems are written to evoke intensity. He has been writing from age 14 and has self-published five prior books – anthologies of erotic and sensual poetry called EROTIC and SEDUCTION, collections of shorter, poignant poems in OFFERING and QUOTES OF PASSION, and his first novel, MAKE IT RAINE. They are all currently available online in different stores, such as Barnes & Noble.

In 2011, Robert entered the National Independence Festival of Creative Arts (NIFCA), the national arts festival of his native Barbados with three poems – Luscious, Rain, and Goblet. All three of the poems achieved awards – Luscious received a silver award, and Goblet and Rain received bronze awards. He also received the **Most Promising Poet** award for the year.

In 2012, Robert entered NIFCA again and one of his poems – Tribute – received a bronze award. Again, in 2016, Robert entered NIFCA and his poem Naniki: Frank Collymore Hall 2016 received a bronze award.

The winning NIFCA entries have been published in the Winning Words anthology produced by the National Cultural Foundation (NCF), the producers of NIFCA.

Another one of his poems Tribute (A Call to Action), which was inspired by the documentary Cultures of Resistance, was highlighted by the Cultures of Resistance producers on their Facebook page.

Robert has also been the featured writer on the Seawoman's Caribbean Writing Opps blog,

His work has been published in an anthology of poetry written by Ainsley Carter, A Journey Into the Abyss of the Mind.

Several of his poems have also been accepted into the St. Somewhere Caribbean E-zine for publication and The Caribbean Writer.

Robert has performed at Love, Poetry and Song 2013 doing one of his love poems, Intimate.

Robert has been a featured poet on UNMUTED INK, an online radio show hosted on WKPJB – The Indie Storm on BlogTalkRadio.com. His recorded interview has been downloaded and listened to over 3000 times. He has also been featured on Ms Jewcee's Erotic Chat, another BlogTalk Radio.com online show.

More recently, he has also been interviewed by Sapphire JBlue on her BlogTalk show Conversations with Sapphire JBlue He has recently been the Author of the Month on The Erotic Book Review blog and the same website has given his novel MAKE IT RAINE four stars

Robert's first two books EROTIC and OFFERING were published in 2014, and his third anthology SEDUCTION was published February 2015. His fourth anthology QUOTES OF PASSION was published in 2016, and his first novel MAKE IT RAINE was released in 2017. They were all re-released in 2023.

www.ingramcontent.com/pod-product-compliance
Lightning Source LLC
LaVergne TN
LVHW061618070526
838199LV00078B/7335